**salmon**poetry

# DEMETER DOES NOT REMEMBER

## MARY MADEC

Published in 2014 by
Salmon Poetry
Cliffs of Moher, County Clare, Ireland
Website: www.salmonpoetry.com
Email: info@salmonpoetry.com

ISBN 978-1-908836-31-1

COVER IMAGE: *The Silent Hunger* by Charlotte Kelly. Oil on canvas. Reproduced
with the kind permission of the artist. www.charlottekelly.com
COVER DESIGN & TYPESETTING: *Siobhán Hutson*
*Printed in Ireland by Sprint Print*

*Salmon Poetry gratefully acknowledges the support of*
*The Arts Council / An Chomhairle Ealaoín*

# Acknowledgments

Acknowledgements to the editors of the following publications in which some of these poems have appeared: *Poetry Ireland, Cyphers, The Stand, Orbis, The Recorder, The Clifden Anthology 2012, The SHOp, Burning Bush 2, The Galway Review, Skylight47, Crannóg.*

# Contents

# Persephone: Coming of Age

At the end of Spring, she plays in the ragged grasses
clumpy, uneven, wet like the hairs on the mount of Venus,

the sentinel peaks rising in the distance
by the tender early light, now her breasts.

In the waters of the inlets her arms and legs
stretch like promontories.

She is aware of the suck and tug of the earth
taking her into itself, into its dark folds.

When she thinks of her hips, they are a boat
carved out of an old apple tree she remembers.

She longs for a river; she would give herself to its bed,
its mud and stones like flesh and bones.

And she knows, as a salmon knows, that she would go with it
into the dark places water flows, on its way to the sea.

# Playing House

The pines to the North
bare bottomed, lanky,
rusty needles on the ground,
cones scattered—
No point going deep
into the middle of that grove
too easily seen from every side;
no point playing house in there.

I go instead to the double birch hedge
by the orchard, its canopy thick in summer,
in winter tremulous,
half-buried bits and pieces
of delph, blue and brown bottles.
I get stones to designate spaces,
assign rooms; light dappling through
the small leaf separations;
with the birds I gather twigs,
sit in my raggle-taggle cave and imagine
life in that dark place
with something unnamable
away from civilization;
I listen to the seasons,
Winter's quiet, Spring's crescendo of determination,
Summer's satisfied hum;
the smell of earth under the first primrose,
in the moist darkness, always cool
in the undergrowth.

I make a home
and those who come
only come on invitation;
now, their votives still glow.
I fashion it from nothing

like a goddess who knows
how homes are made,
who knows that's what a goddess makes
from her hidden stores.

When I leave, it comes with me,
emergency shelter, a shrine,
a reliquary of childhood,
to which I return to find
with those eyes again
beauty flashing like mother-of-pearl
out of the darkness.

# Apple Tree

I stood sturdy outside your back door in Winter,
blushed pink in the Spring,

gave my limbs to your summer games,
my leaves to your memories.

Now as you snap twigs and hug black trunks
in an orchard I do not know

you might remember a time when lichens
did not grow on my bark,

a red-and-yellow snap-apple time
where I swayed in the breeze.

I was your cradle in Summer
and before Winter,
my apples came tumbling down to your feet.

# The Frosted Puddle

glints first, then, glistens
as the sun begins to polish it

crackles as the sun splinters it
underfoot.  Then, fills

suddenly to its lip
with water.  Like an eye brims

makes clear
why you were footsore

by the time you were done with it.

# What Does a Body Remember?

The heat of a slap or an icy hand
somewhere it shouldn't be?
You tell me it's my pineal gland
not doing its job in joining
what Descartes called a body and soul.
So I carry them along both
as if they do not know each other
as if I hopped out of my body
when it got too cold
and curled into some corner of the universe,
onto some star in the Nebula of Adromeda,
and looked down at what I was
wishing for.

It's part of the game to go into the body
and tame its lunacy, its insane needs
to be held and caressed
to take like a favourite animal
what you need, lying down.
And not to even wish for words.
To give your body
to some other body
your back arching into total abandon
as you hold the flanks of the darkness
and forget how you couldn't bear the light.
That is what you remember.
That is what you would like to forget,
how the light stung you,
mocked you,
forced you to see your shadow
and be afraid of it.

# Pinhole

*"Were I able to shut my eyes, ears, legs,*
*hands and walk into myself for a thousand years*
*Perhaps I would reach – I do not know its name – what matters most"*

ANNA SWIR

You invited me into that space,
between what you were thinking and what you said,
and my heart paced up and down.

For I knew that it was also the space
between the holding of hands
and the long embrace.

I could hear the rain,
its random punctuation,
commas on my thoughts but never full stops,
my life spilling through its interludes.

Now through the pinhole of memory
I reassemble the room,
the chair on which we sat,
the table, the open book.

# Breaking the Horses

Time keeps our secrets.
The dark horses which bolted
in the night now stand calmly
with the white steeds of the morning
who will never know
the shadow of what went before.

The mirror here saw
what happened.
And what is happening now.
The ache, the heartbreak
which it holds
as I look back into it,

the memories shivering, whinnying.

# Almanac

*"I am the Angel who says Remember"*

E. Ní Chuilleanáin

Remember the wood sorrel under the pines,
Spring lifting the leaves into a green luminosity;
between your teeth its liquid light;

The dog rose on the ditches in May
spreading in all directions,
its perfume, delicate, tender, its thorns unforgiving;

The nectar of fuschia
drawn by your pursed lips
assessed like wine by the height of sun
in July;

the vetches after the blue flowers
turn to caviar in August;
you  played with their black beads,
these miniature peas, an acquired taste;

black sloes, shrivelled and pungent
hit the roof of your mouth,
cut like the slant of October light
and coming Winter.

You were tuned once to these rhythms,
knew from when you saw frogspawn in the drains
that the seasons would tumble into your lap as gifts
you'd be sorting in a bed-sit in centre city
sifting from the chaff of the years, the memories
of angels.

# The Little Girl Sleeps

in a field of Archangels—
bright yellow flowers in whorls on erect stems,
upper lips hooded
lower lips streaked red-brown—
content in this herb of Venus,
her little white thighs bare
where her dress has risen up.

You see her in the recesses of your mind,
in among things you remember,
you kneel before her
with tenderness as if touching
knowledge too deep for the mind,

spread-eagled to the sun,
she waits for a kiss on her lips
like a dew-drop to wake her up
but you hold back, afraid.

For if she wakes, she will find herself
struggling with you out of bed
the stretches of growth, the strains of age
the disfigured skin of your thighs
and she might weep

not as a child weeps expecting love.
She might weep to see the burnt field,
stones and gravel taking over
the once luscious hedgerow,
how your red-rimmed eyes grieve –

Could you bear to see her wake up to that?

# Tumble

I land in you unexpectedly,
down and something silky like new grass
scattering
and it is  soft and I fit perfectly
like in memory foam
and maybe it is a memory
and it is silky like a caress, your fingers
stroking me
and new, I have never come here before
and green somehow like soft summer
warming me
down deeper than I have ever known
and maybe you heard the whimper
as I gave myself to
the comfort of you concave
as a moon but not cold or blue
and I gave myself as a child
extends her little arms wide
and trusting on the world
the edge between inside and outside
blurred like tears blur
eyes that still see
and your arms wrap around me
and I am satisfied.

# Picnic

We spread out the cloth,
smiles across the squares
as we planned deft moves
for our imaginary chessmen
over the soft Spring earth
pungent after a shower.
The sun warmed
two blades of grass
in the slant of March
and pink-eared *bellis perennis*
held sturdy in the breeze.

# Hades

You, Zeus of the departed
were vigorous and passionate
and when your shadow crossed the green
where Peresephone was last seen
playing daisy chains as girls do
you couldn't resist, could you?

She was uneasy at first
when she knew she had already fallen
into the dark slit of the earth.
But you came up tops.
She saw that you were the mystery man
she was hell-bent on.

Below she recognized how stereotypes restrict vision
and once her eyes were accustomed
was surprised by your warm blue flesh.
Queen of the dark she strolled in the underworld
with Cerberus, your pet dog.

Only in the fields of Asphodel did she weep
where the neither hot nor cold, neither good nor bad people
who took no chances, roam, never get to meet.
Who now look at her in the distance
bedevilled by her courage, the jingle of her jewels.
They suffer looking back for what might have been.

# Hades to Persephone

Your hand is so close it could touch mine
but you pull it away in time
tracing the boundary

any closer and I step
into your shadow
you into mine

and rather than disrupt
affection's awkward reach
we play at catch the plural pronoun,

go round and round each
of our language islands,
eddies of meaning in the delta.

This vertigo of words
could throw us into each other's arms,
leave us confused

about how to distribute
endings on verbs,
as their tense, their mood come to light.

# Persephone to Hades

You say that skin is a vast and temporary shelter
so we construct a scaffold of words
to reach each other,
a sturdy syntax for our sounds,

long and short lines in iambic pentameter,
pulsing in a diastole and systole of our consonants,
ripped vowels looking for sensual measure,
our lips precipices.

My hands are cold as we walk out at night
admiring trees you say you have never seen so tall.
This eloquent, elusive evening light
understates, fades in the undergrowth,
to the vague outlines of the road.

If desire has a shape
it is betrayed by the distance between us,
and the dance of atoms in that space,
words which track thoughts we cannot yet share;
sibilants and sonorants hang softly in the air.

# First Kiss

*"Maybe this is what a friend means*
*When she says there is a pair of lips*
*In the air, maybe this is desire and need too"*
    MARK COX

Those lips in the air, move like velvet and sponge
to make words, round vowels,
explode plosives into the quiet morning;

backed by gutturals they do the labial stuff
your tongue peeping to clean them off
and reward them for their work with a lick of approval;

the angle in your eye which brings your gaze to mine
sends my lips off to float too like a red line
in a white sky, a kite let loose on a summer's day.

You put your fingers up to cover them
as if to hide your secret intention,
as if to restore them back on your face

and my lips on mine;
a pause for thought, a breath—
not ready yet for that first kiss.

# On This One Single Night

My hands have the same blood as the Spring.
The coolness of early morning.
The heat of my neck
hit by the frisson of your lips.
My shoulder cuffs pitched in the cave of your chest.
And what is this,
your heavy head now against my breast?
Then a kiss on the ivories, pianoforte,
a ripple of soft notes on your teeth.
Our hands catch the edge of light
on the waves, bring us to beach,
like confused whales.
We wake on the sand to madness.
The sad and lonely pitch of a love cry.

# Why Was Demeter Surprised

Persephone liked the underworld?
She knew the waters of the inner earth,
the ribbons of rain that wove
through the first curls of Persephone's hair.

Like every mother she could recall
the butterfly bubbles Persephone made,
as she swam with the algae of her womb,
clutched the ferns of the uterine wall
in a current of amnion, waves rushing at her throat.

In the darkness of Demeter,
Persephone happily opened her mouth like a fish,
undaunted.  Outside, she needed
Demeter to lick the blood from her heels, her thighs,
wipe the darkness from her head, her eyes.

Demeter must have known somewhere
in her long life, in the strata of less,
the promise of warmth,
how sun often comes
through some regretful crevice,

in that moment of seeing her daughter
her little face turning red in the stinging light,
she pulled away from her likeness,
her blue eyes.

# Persephone to Demeter

After Demeter's *Prayer to Hades* by Rita Dove

Mum, give us a break!
What I wish for you
that you stop
putting your old head
on our young shoulders.

You are right that no one shows faith
in anything without dying
but you seem not to see
that coming here has been that
for me.

Leave Hades alone.
We still remember the sky,
Even if it's a hue of purple
we see in each other's eyes.
We mirrors do not tell lies.
What I see of myself now in Hades
brings new life; Mum, I will come back

And you will wear your floral dress
and we will dance
with joy over the fields
knowing exactly how to look after
the lives we change.
Responsible and amazed.

# Mnemonic

In the secret of my heart
a garden in late bloom

I pick a hardy rose
give it to you.

In the stillness of November
so much to remember.

# Demeter Does Not Remember

Persephone, her shadowed daughter
in the portico, peeping through the cracked wall.
Or what she said to keep her away.

Or what she gave her to dam her legs
when blood flowed,
red into the underworld.

Demeter cannot remember her first smile or teeth,
the words she made.
Persephone would have liked to know.

Now, a woman, she looks into the still lake of her dreams,
filled by the purlings of the Styx.
What does she see?

She walks away heartbroken
from the quivering reflection.
Cries out, 'Demeter is not me.'

# Bound

She took the pomegranate seeds unwittingly
the meal of strength Hades served up
before she went back to her mother.

On her tongue something happened
which bound her to him
could not be undone,

his seed in hers
and hers in him
growing inexorably to light

where one sees into the heart
the grains of happiness
measured against the dark.

Once ripe, its copious harvest
spills from the corm—
the joy

that the long beloved
who was once a stranger
is imprinted there forever.

# Hades Said, "Go!"

back to your mother
to the land you came from.
Up through the slit in the ground.
Wipe the night from your eyes,
find the girl you left behind
among the flowers,
her wounds still smarting.
Bring her back with you
to me.

But love her first,
she has the secret of how
our wounds explode
into roses,
their perfume everywhere.

# Will I Take This Watery Sun?

swallow it into the darkness

as the long shadow
of the hedgerow
searches into me?

I am a bud, which bloomed
too late,
thought your feathery touch
was love

somehow a fool to believe
in the exhilaration
of a pet day.

Now my petals hold back
from your kisses
given in parenthesis

outside all around
your great life
not for

unclosing me

or will you give me back
what I heard
in the darkness

the prose of survival

better than all the trumped up
promises of Spring.?

# So Shall I Live

*After the Book of Ruth*

Your eyes half shut
like windows at dusk

your body open like a lotus

hands meandering
a meditation of sorts

as you trace my contours
onto the walls of your mind

its topography,

the ripe apple of science
plump and tender when I lie on my side,

the rhythm of our breathing
like the wind swaying

the trees on an autumn evening

until I turn over down towards your feet.
Boaz prayed for the woman

who aroused him,
frightened him from his sleep.

When he touched her hair he believed.

I prayed too, thrashing like Ruth
until I found the perfect shelter

my heart wrapped in yours
for better,
for better.

# As Night Falls

Streetlights glint and wink through
the limbs of the old beech tree outside.
I go to hold myself against the bole,
hear the long echo from its dark centre,

wonder if it knows me from when I played
here long ago with the children,
*ring-a-ring-a-rosie* in its shade,
the imprint of the years in its thick bark,

its life too a secret from me,
all those pictures I made in my head
nothing against history, what you might
choose to tell me, word for word, now

how life lived itself in you.

# A Prophecy for Middle Age

Homer has Odysseus set out in his fifties
beyond happy-ever-after
through Hades

as if there he could find
the self he left behind
first time,

his treasured oar now a useless tool
for the new task
and the male badges of his youth,

the bull the boar and the ram
meaningless totems
which the ghost of Tiresias asks him

to sacrifice to the god Neptune
before he crosses back over
to Ithaca to be king.

The next journey, the ghost says
death at last,
to come from the sea.

He sets out again
in mid-life
half crazy, half wise

as if he understood
what this was about
takes on the trials

and humiliation,
necessary searching,
back to the place

from where he started,
insights gasping.

# Plato Records

how in the beginning we were Siamese twins
joined back to back,

our four legs and four arms, touching,
a skin-to-skin of round calves and biceps.

We each looked on the world as we spun,
never allowed to contemplate the fulcrum,

longing to be turned to each other,
my breast upon your ribcage

your arms across my middle back,
our tongues circling the silence and chaos

of head and heart, wondering
what would become of the great unknown

between us,
before we were pulled apart, cursed by the gods,

to spend all of life looking for the perfect union,
searching the world for the other half.

# Soon it will be Winter

and Demeter does not know what she hates most

about the change – her straw hair, her broken nails,

a shrivelling up inside, no blood rain,

insomnia as she tosses her tired head this way and that.

She thinks of Persephone, the daughter she fed

and is jealous of those pert little breasts,

those eyes, reminding her of another bed

where she was desirable as a wife.

She can feel her hardening arteries, her sagging eyes

stretched to crows' feet as she smiles.

There is no sap inside her anymore, a greyness

rising up through  her thighs.


Persephone is wet with smiles

her soft legs parting for Hades.

# Afterthought

Is this age, not knowing
if you are still fit for purpose
when purposes change?

What remains when love is force of habit,
you arrange carefully
forgotten immortelles,

each morning's doily of burnt milk,
the knife wounds on the bread board,
the dry crumbs

remind you that
you value too little ordinary sustenance,
distrust the thin lip of your teacup,

the mouth's need of them,
your embarrassed, tired, empty arms,
your thighs' stiff-boned descent,

the skin falling ever so slightly away
from your arms,
separating muscle and fascia.

If this is wisdom, you think, it is only
the echoes of voices gone
and insight gained which remains.

And blood might interrupt your thoughts
when you tilt your head
so you can't remember,

as you struggle across the river
to the other side of the kitchen.

# Is it Adonis

I embrace?
His warm flesh staid, like
marble.
He stands voluminous and solid
not remotely in need
of my affection.

I throw myself at him,
my eyes stretch
to meet his,
my lips rest
miserably on his cold lips.

I do so want him
to hold my longing
needy heart
towards his
but nothing yields.

So I stand in the sun,
the stinging recognition
of implacable desire
in my eyes
he aloof, indifferent.

Like Ozymandias.
The torment
of lone and level sands.
I am dumbed by the whiteness
of his marble flesh,
his regal silence.

# Why, Demeter

*"I am inhabited by a cry.*
*Nightly it flaps out*
*Looking, with its hooks, for something to love."*

    *Elm,* SYLVIA PLATH

do you hide your face with its wrinkles? Is it fear
because you do not want me to see who you are?

You cover your thoughts with a cloak
and dagger of voice, a false poise

which hurts; and underneath, your hands
sweat and writhe, turn into talons?

Night after night, I fall on the hill and in the hollow,
trip on my will, tangle in the brush of earth as I try to follow

you. But you let me down,
leave me in the sun to burn, in the rain to drown.

Now I fear how stupefied and insensible I will become
deciphering the hieroglyphs of your tomb.

I stand here alone, unable to share my insights,
a stone for my pillow, in my hand a wish bone

from some insubstantial bird whose song is sung,
its feathers scattered, its neck wrung.

I cannot see what cast the shadow on the ground.
Will it pass as it should, or will it scream out loud?

# Grave

*"It is tragic to be a poet now
And not a lover
Paradised under the mutest bough"*

*April Dusk*, PATRICK KAVANAGH

Little by little the worms come out and feast
on her flesh, bore her bones, slide over
remembered sensations,

how hands felt at the moment of touch
tongues in the coldness of their faces
how nipples rose and juices flowed.

Is this what it means to go back where you came from?
*Did she ever dream of being Mother Earth?*
*Did she ever dream of grass for her hair?*

The wedding veil now a gauze
to bandage the running sore
of disappointed love, of love that tried,

of love that hung like whispers in the breeze
but the grasses tremble to remind
him of what lies underneath—


something died.

# My Dear Hades

Something about you reminds me
of mussels on the rocks,
black–blue clumps of darkness
rising and falling in this new harbour.

What is the smell, inhaled
as something healthy now,
better than hypnotic narcissi?

The wind is calm enough
for me to appreciate my breath
is taken.  It is you
I am breathing in and out.

Your blue flesh beneath my hands
in fronds of wrack.
Small fertile vesicles burst open
soften the old bones.

Mostly we float around
except when you scuba dive to see
what you remember from below.

When the sun comes we lie belly up
our fingers in touch
as we listen to molluscs gurgling
under water, enchanted, satisfied.

# Too Early for an Oracle

I have to stay here longer, I now know,
weigh each fateful consequence
of my words against your silence,
explore the metaphors we made
to enclose us,
test the images we reflect back.

Do they have doors
we can open so we can escape?
Or can we live in them and breathe?
And what of the symbols in the dark?
They fall like dominoes
helpless consecutive prayers.

You say you don't want the apple
and you take the single arm-chair.

# In Love with the Greeks

Recall how Eros, minion and constant companion to Aphrodite
for all his mischief was incomplete,
needing Himeros—desire— to give him wings,
and Anteros—love's reciprocal—for the rebound;
this is how he keeps the balance on Aphrodite's scales.

This dream is disturbing.  You are sitting naked
surrounded by a man-made fence,
your genitals displayed
as if you are reaching for a chamber pot,
certainly not stretching out to a lover.

Remember how Himeros and Anteros were youths
and the Greeks knew how age steals them away,
leaves Eros in his bed alone,
to complain of lack of libido, erectile dysfunction,
enlarged prostate,

Aphrodite at the height of her game, disappointed,
knowing at last her G-spot,
her clitoris trembling without shame.
Himeros weak and old
Anteros, stiff and cold.

# The Problem Demeter

is that one learns to love again
by loving.
And being loved.

When you see Persephone
in you
rather than the other way round.

And you find yourself charmed
by another Hades
attending at the shrine of your breasts

telling  you over and over
how beautiful you are,
his large hand coaxing the old fluids.

This too is a kind of dying
the way you begin again
to implant the earth with your wisdom.

Now that you've cracked the code
of your binary notation
you'll never grow old.

# Zeus, You are Too White For Me

standing there in the sure light
of your importance.
So bright I cannot see your eyes.
You wave your hands ceremoniously
this way and that as if to say
you told me so.

I'd feel more secure if you showed me
you are sometimes unsure
and wonder if anyone could get
what I'm going through,
I wasn't asking you to explain anything
just hoping you'd put your arms around me,

tell me that my little life was worth everything,
that you understood how hard it is to fail
at what you've worked hardest at,
that you get the pain
of seeing your life swirl
into the rings of the moon

your tired dizzy words
which mean nothing now,
seek out the lips of someone old and wise,
the eyes of someone who has seen it all.
Zeus, that could not be me.

# Dare

Demeter, to go with Persephone to the underworld,
see her embrace the darkness you fear,
the half-lights of Hades in her hair,
on her face, joy of love found.

Was it you, Demeter, who sent her underground?
You, her mother who could not bear to see her heart in light of day
as she picked flowers wondering what forces
from below the earth made them grow.

Now when your daughter comes back to you
in the Spring sun,
you regret that you fought with her
even if she is no longer an innocent girl.

She went there because of you,
discovered to her surprise
that darkness is food
like water and clay for roots.

# On the Cobbles of Hell

you to and fro as I fall asleep
the pattern you make
a hopscotch of *hello goodbye*
*yes no always never.*

You breathe into me,
a kiss in contest,
yet my breath hits
only the cold air.

I stretch out my hands to you.
Where else can I go?
I throw the pebble
hop along the shore.

When we get to where we're supposed to be
I am confused
by the formless sand,
its fine sparkling mica.

If that were Jesus the Prophet
who took my hand
he was sifting something,
extolling in detail
its fine particles through his fingers.

# In a True Dialogue

you give up another bit of yourself
to trust

some fractured truth
to say what a heart is
or a soul, my mind or yours
these labels past their sell-by-date

nothing for once and for all.
however carefully thought out
the vows were then
and now what are these words

uttered so tenderly
and will you remember
the campanula and the tormentil
we gathered in the meadow last Spring?

I balance like an old ballerina
fear what comes after this long pirouette.

# They Sit on the Edge of the World

on a ledge of granite,
laugh that it could be a chaise
and I see them lean in towards each other

the way a hip roof pulls its walls in a prayer
this soft shelter they latch securely
with their hands, one on one

his reliable steady heart beat
like a pendulum clock
the metronome of their thoughts

the sough of the sea
ringing in their ears
the whisper of moving limpets

I can see their eyes mesmerized
by the pinkest sea-thrift
in clefts of bare rock

bold and beautiful
against the odds.

# When the Storm is Over

I am steeped in scree.
Something has fallen away
and you who come to help me
trespass to save me,

my heart already weeping, sliced
by prophecies; and not even your songs
in honeyed partitions can soothe
the raucous crows at the window.

I struggle for foothold on the unsteady boards
even the walls fall away from my leaning
and I see the holes in the roof overhead
as the sky darkens to charcoal.

I am inside and outside this moment
beyond mantras and patience,
putting the knives of the morning
safely into the shaking drawer,

you still there waiting to see
what I'll do next
wondering if I'll throw a rope
to hold myself against the headwall

or exit.

# Hello Dem or is it Perseph?

Hades here, the man with hands
which hold other hands but not as if
each of them was the only one
in the world. Know what I mean?
Better, my dear Cerberus,
to disclose my strange ways to the ladies
and how I walk with multiple leads
champing

Still I will concede that I cannot multi-task
even with all these hands.
And if I'm honest I want to tell you
I forgot what my hand feels like
until you stretched out yours to me
and said 'Hello Mr Hades!'

It was blue and cold,
you took it from under my glove
and I felt such heat – hell I did!
And I do believe it came from beneath
your fingers, your cheeks aglow.

I didn't know hands
might search like this
for where palms meet plump and tender
measuring up against each other.

Hey girl, someone should have told me
this could happen
before that first handshake was over.
Hello.

# Love: An Assay

Forensic questions first, said the Ghost
Are there two experiments
or one? Here are the results

of the titration. The course of fluids
measures hearts.
The residue,
the salt, what each is worth.

So you think you have worked it out, said the Ghost
but what if the new outpouring
does not come
from the same source?

Beyond the protocols
of laboratories,
the pros and cons
of holding hands.

Look for the ratio of friend to lover, said the Ghost.
Measure the circles of
feather fingers, length of gaze,
eyelid flicker.

Sit in a corner,
watch for the ways
they settle in
to shared idiom.

Are you seriously asking me to take down, write up
what makes the deepest
most vulnerable place quiver
ache and be consoled?

And is that love? said the Ghost
Tell me, is that love? I say.

Between these two rivers, said the Ghost
you stand in the cold.
You have to swim

to where you are going,
your destiny not in evidence
in this assay.

# At the End of Summer

you remain,
like the imprint of a body in the sand,
the mistral whipping the lines away.

In the mirror I see the impression you made
my eyes brighter,
smiling back at me.

Your casual words now, no doubt forgotten.
What-ifs tease on the edge of my thoughts,
soften on my lips.

I still see your smile propped by two white cups
you are bringing back to the kitchen
after our mint tea.

Now the mistral has blown my shirt away
smacks sand on my back, groans like winter,
in the evening pretends to be dark and menacing.

I struggle with my snack.
Apricots are easily broken in two at this ripeness.
If you were here I would offer you half.

On the white plate, the apricot.
The blush of the sun still visible
on its downy skin.

# If Salt Loses its Taste

what can make it salty again?
If we jumped into the ocean
dripped dry like mer people
would it cover us with a salty residue
we could lick off?

Our tears and sweat,
what might come
from bubbly vesicles, mucosa,
we could spread
like an unction with our tongues.

And what of the chemistry of tears,
would the sea sting our briny eyes
or would it help us to recognise
our wet weather-beaten heads
bobbing like loosened buoys?

The sea might be worth its salt.
Its long call like the blackback's
ricochets off the crests
of the waves,
its vowels crash on the shore.

Will you give it your secrets, answer
to its open mouth?
Its horizon changes as the earth rotates.
Its tides tumble in on the equinox.

Put your hands out.
Give your whole body to it
like a prayer, a libation.
There is no other way.

# All Around Us

After Jane Hirschfield, *Each Happiness Ringed by Lions*

There were lions circling today
tails twitching
as if the nerves connected
to some overworked synapses,

heads menacingly to the ground,
fierce eyes focusing on us
waiting for the moment
to pounce.

We lie still in the long grass
our hearts safe from their gaze,
and when night comes we are grateful
for spears of light shooting from the sky

to show us  the way,
out there, somewhere
beyond the galaxies

the lions asleep
while we make pace
with our dreams.

# Autumn Evening

Now I wonder why I kept telling Demeter to go,
that she had my permission,
why I ever thought it was mine to give.
I was the midwife for her soul,
coaching her through the labour
of breathing, her lungs filling up
like a tidal pool full of seaweed.

I gave myself to the intimacy
of her clammy hand and her sweaty head
on the pillow; somehow it seemed
like I was wiping up a great athlete
on the homerun
I didn't think very much of how it would be
when it was all over

as one thinks little of the closing of day,
the sun slanting through the window
from behind the alder
the wind rising, the leaves trembling
the darkness chasing all living creatures
in search for comfort.
*It will come. It will,* I tell myself
Which is why I said, *Go!*

# After This Ebb

should I depend on the sea
coming back in over the sand?

I try to understand your words:
*You open me like an oyster*
*sometimes with a sharp knife*
*sometimes with the gentle rise of the tide.*

I too long for the tugs and gurgles
of silky water in around my feet

flowing in finally
over the rocks
leaving me waist-high.
in the healing saline.

The crisped wrack swells
into all the recesses of the shore.

I swim with the fronds in my fingers,
vesicles interlocked,
ripe fruit ready
to burst open
like you.

And what now are these tears,
this salty water in my throat
as you open
me?

# Heads or Tails

*He loves me*
*He loves me not*
Will I toss a coin or
pull the petals of the daisy
one by one?

He looks at me as if I carry
the elusive nectar of desire        *loves me*
He looks into a mesmerizing screen
oblivious of what I need          *loves me not*

Each petal I pull is a fear
of what will become
of us

Each petal I pull is a dream

The petals one by one
confetti or tears
Will I stay or run?

Have I prayed for heads?
I toss the golden centre
into the breeze.

# Taking off the Eye Mask

Response to Levertov's *Eye Mask*

When I think I am ready, I see your hand fall
idly over my face,
I feel the soft hold of your fingers
barely touching.

You peep beneath black silk
as if you are taking hair out of my eyes.
I hear you say I have no need
of its shelter anymore.

I am open, the gauze yet to go
and still vulnerable, but know your eyes
which meet mine
draw out my darkness.

It is simple after all: I feel my face
when you gaze upon me,
as if the maze my mind makes
finds a dénouement in your words.
I don't need to hide anymore.

# Demeter: Coming of Age

As I bathe alone, I wonder
what would be a good outcome.

This time I let my head
below the level of the water

and my hair spreads out
like thong-weed in the sea.

My middle-aged body lops
and the water makes

tides around my hips
and breasts.

My legs with their varicose veins
the legacy of maternity
I embrace

I let it all hang out.
It makes no difference now
that this man or that

loved this body
rested on it like summer sun
on grass.

Just as the grass barely notices
the creatures who crawl on the earth

just as the earth itself is indifferent
to movements on its surface

waits for boiling magma
to rise up to its thin skin.

It will take something like this
to shift the tectonic plates
reunite the old continents.

# Yours

I write best from an old nest I built in your ear
my darkness warmed by you,

I am not shy in there as I ruffle my nakedness,
unaware of my infirmities.

My darkness is not darkness to you
and when I am strong my light too is yours,

our gaze best held in the fractional
break-up of light and dark

mellowing our features and what the years have done
to all of us, what the years do.

But besides these lines, there is the gift
of insight that comes only with time,

snap of twigs woven into stray soft wool
from black and white sheep,

words that are spoken before the courage
comes to write them down,

because they are your words as they are mine,
which for reasons unknown, I get to compose.

You, who know my heart
my light too is yours.

# So We Share Words

The letters jump out in animation
fall like Scrabble letters
flat on the table, looking like
they'll make nothing.

I wonder what I can say
in the confines of squares,
how I might triple my best score
aiming to be clever though not apt

enough to know how to fill
the interstices of silences
where I play out all the dramas
of self construction

when I catch you, smiling
as new words form, promising
to be sturdy and upright,
scaffolding for the bits of you

that seep through, like a smile,
like what you might confide,
what you might share
if you get these words right.

# Threshold

You are standing in the door smiling,
wondering perhaps if you'll come in.
I know you see everything,
my life spread out in the shadows
so I look up at you, thankful for your deference,
your averting eye.

I'm smiling too,
thankful that you stopped by,
uncomfortable
I wasn't better prepared,
haven't my house in order,
ashamed of my chaos:
my clothes on the floor,
notes on everything I'm going to do
pinned on the walls,
my unintelligible books,
and words for poems
hanging in the air.

You might ask how anything
works around here.
I know you're not like that.
You just stand and smile,
the best picture in the house
framed by the door.

Then it occurs to me as I look at you
silhouetted in the light
that you are waiting for me.
You're here to invite
me to take what I need,
get out.

# Diptych

If I were an artist I'd draw Demeter looking back,
Persephone stretching out like a light beam
into Spring.

Demeter like Lot's wife
shadows in the salt,
her strained moist eyes

bright as the candle of winter
flickering on the thin outline of herself,
the white x-ray of her bones,

pale tissue in which throbs her dreams—
out of which come her sobs and screams.
Persephone comes back to Demeter

with her old juices,
claims her so she might live,
dollops of tears, Swarovskis on lupins.

# Forecast

You turn me around and change the frame.
You're sorry and winded.

There's some awkward readjustment of limbs,
like trees that find their branches
when the wind dies down.

We go back the way we came, the cloud breaking up
as it comes in from the sea.

Everything from this angle looks different,
you take out your thermometer,
barometer, wind vane:

*The outlook is good*, you say:
*Cumulonimbus calvus*, your favourite,

a sky filled with narrative,
great big faces puffed,
playfully portentous.

You say they will be tipped
with red and gold at sunset.

MARY MADEC is Director of Villanova University's Study Abroad Program in Ireland. She has a Ph.D in Linguistics from The University of Pennsylvania, U.S.A. She has published in Ireland, Britain and the USA, and in 2008 won The Hennessy XO Award for Emerging Poetry. Her first collection, *In Other Words*, was published by Salmon Poetry in 2010 and in 2012 she edited a book of poems *Jessica Casey & Other Works* (also from Salmon Poetry) from the award-winning community writing project Away With Words collective which she co-founded in 2008.